$20.00

861827

WEATHERWISE

DOPPLER RADAR, SATELLITES, and COMPUTER MODELS

| The Science of WEATHER FORECASTING |

Paul Fleisher

LERNER PUBLICATIONS COMPANY · MINNEAPOLIS

Lerner Publications Company
A division of Lerner Publishing Group, Inc.
241 First Avenue North
Minneapolis, MN 55401 U.S.A.

Website address: www.lernerbooks.com

Library of Congress Cataloging-in-Publication Data

Fleisher, Paul.
     Doppler radar, satellites, and computer models : the science
of weather forecasting / by Paul Fleisher.
        p.   cm. — (Weatherwise)
     Includes bibliographical references and index.
     ISBN 978–0–8225–7535–1 (lib. bdg. : alk. paper)
     1. Weather forecasting—Juvenile literature. I. Title.
QC995.43.F54 2011
551.63—dc22   2009044919

Manufactured in the United States of America
1 – PC – 7/15/10

CONTENTS

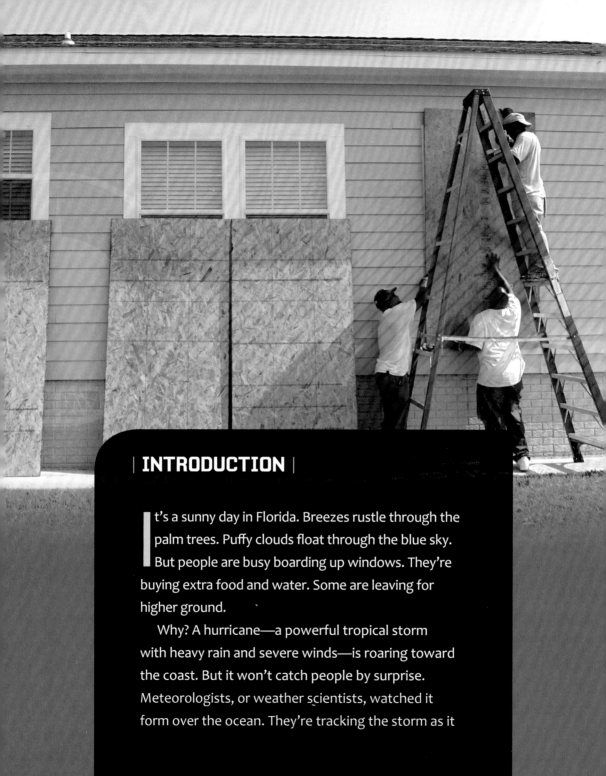

| INTRODUCTION |

It's a sunny day in Florida. Breezes rustle through the palm trees. Puffy clouds float through the blue sky. But people are busy boarding up windows. They're buying extra food and water. Some are leaving for higher ground.

Why? A hurricane—a powerful tropical storm with heavy rain and severe winds—is roaring toward the coast. But it won't catch people by surprise. Meteorologists, or weather scientists, watched it form over the ocean. They're tracking the storm as it travels. Their warnings could save hundreds of lives and millions of dollars in damage.

FORECASTING THE WEATHER

Weather is the condition of Earth's atmosphere—the layer of air that surrounds the planet—at any certain time. Forecasters look at weather over time to make predictions, or forecasts, for the days or weeks ahead.

Weather affects people's lives. For instance, heavy rain or snow can make driving dangerous. Storms can cause airlines to cancel flights. Bad weather can damage electric lines and shut down electric power. Weather affects crops too. Farmers must prepare for storms or dry spells.

Passengers waited in New York's Kennedy Airport for delayed flights during a snow storm in 2007.

Banks of computer screens show different types of weather information to help meteorologists make forecasts.

People check forecasts to learn what problems are on the way. Weather forecasts can save lives. Forecasters can protect livelihoods.

Forecasting is helpful even when the weather is not extreme. Everyone wants to know what kind of weather to expect. Should we wear heavy coats to school or work? Will we need umbrellas and raincoats?

Forecasters need to know three things to make a prediction. First, they need to know about current conditions. What kinds of weather are happening around the world?

Second, they need to know how the weather is changing. The air around Earth moves, bringing changing weather conditions. Distant weather may be heading closer. Which way is the wind blowing?

Is the temperature rising or falling? Is the amount of moisture in the air changing? What about air pressure—the force of air pressing down on Earth? Is it rising or falling?

Third, forecasters need to understand weather patterns. What kind of weather is common in a certain area? Which wind patterns bring fair weather? Where do storms usually develop?

Answering these questions gives a good idea of what the coming weather will be. Let's find out how scientists collect and use information to make accurate forecasts.

CHAPTER ONE
GATHERING WEATHER INFORMATION

Suppose you wanted to predict the weather for your area. Your first step would be to observe. You'd keep track of each day's weather.

You might take measurements several times a day. You'd record the temperature. You'd measure air pressure and humidity (the amount of moisture in the air). You'd measure the day's rainfall or snowfall. You would study the clouds overhead. You'd record the wind speed and direction. Before long, you'd start to see patterns.

Some days you might see thick, puffy cumulus clouds building up early in the morning. You'd notice that thundershowers often happen on those days. On other days, you might see layered stratus clouds getting thicker. You'd find that steady rain or snow often follows those clouds.

You might discover something about wind direction. In most of North America, when the wind blows from the northwest, the air is usually cool and dry. When the wind blows from the

WIND VANES SHOW WHICH DIRECTION THE WIND IS BLOWING. THE WIND WOULD PUSH AGAINST THE PIG DECORATION ON TOP OF THIS WIND VANE TO TURN IT.

southeast, the air is warm and humid. Rain is more likely on those days.

The more information you collected, the more you'd know what to expect. And the better your forecasts could be. Soon you'd become an expert about local weather. You could look at one day's measurements and make a good guess about the next day.

The first step in forecasting is to gather information. That's what meteorologists do. They use the most high-tech equipment to take local measurements. And they get other weather data (information) from all around the world.

Weather predictions have gotten much better since the mid-1900s. Why? The main reason is technology. Modern meteorologists use satellites—machines that circle Earth in space—to watch the weather. Meteorologists also use radar. This device uses radio waves to see moisture moving through the air from many miles away. Finally, meteorologists use powerful computers to collect and process weather data.

THE EQUIPMENT ON BOARD THIS AIRPLANE HELPS METEOROLOGISTS GATHER INFORMATION ABOUT WEATHER CONDITIONS AND EVENTS. THIS SPECIALLY DESIGNED PLANE CAN SAFELY FLY INTO HURRICANES TO COLLECT STORM DATA.

In the United States, the National Weather Service (NWS) is in charge of weather analysis. The NWS is a government agency. Its job is to observe and predict the weather. Collecting weather information is a huge task. The job never ends. It goes on twenty-four hours a day, every day of the year.

MEASURING FROM EARTH'S SURFACE

Weather stations gather information about the weather at Earth's surface. The NWS operates 121 weather stations around the country. Each station has a complete set of instruments for measuring and recording weather conditions. Stations report their findings to the NWS four times a day.

Instruments at weather stations include thermometers to measure temperature. Hygrometers measure humidity. Anemometers measure wind speed, and wind vanes show wind direction. Air pressure is measured with barometers. Rain gauges measure rainfall. Weather stations also identify the kinds of clouds overhead.

NWS stations are hundreds of miles apart. In between stations, the weather might be quite different from conditions at the nearest station. Weather varies even between nearby places. For example, conditions on a hilltop can be very different from weather in the valley below. A city may be several degrees hotter than the nearby countryside. So the NWS stations still leave a lot of weather unrecorded.

Fortunately, many other places collect weather data too. Airports have weather stations. Weather buoys collect data as they float in the ocean. Ships at sea send reports to the NWS. So do airplanes in flight. Thousands of weather stations across the United States take measurements automatically.

This National Weather Service (NWS) office is in Shreveport, Louisiana. The structure behind the building holds radar instruments.

Stations all over the world also gather weather information. The United States and 187 other countries belong to the World Meteorological Organization (WMO). The WMO member countries have more than ten thousand weather stations. Each sends out reports four times a day. They send information to WMO weather centers in the United States, Australia, the United Kingdom, and Russia. Thousands of ocean buoys, ships, and planes around the world also send reports to the WMO.

Still, weather reports miss much of Earth's weather. Most of the ocean has no weather reporting at the surface. And polar regions have very few weather stations.

THIS WEATHER BALLOON IS READY FOR TAKEOFF FROM THE NWS STATION IN BOISE, IDAHO.

MEASURING AT A DISTANCE

Meteorologists also gather weather information from great distances. Certain instruments help them do this job. Each NWS station sends up a weather balloon twice a day. The balloon rises into the upper atmosphere. It carries a small package of instruments called a radiosonde.

As the balloon rises, the radiosonde measures temperature, humidity, winds, and air pressure. It sends information back to the station by radio. The process is called taking a sounding. Weather stations take soundings at the same times each day all around the world.

About 20 miles (32 kilometers) up, the balloon bursts. The radiosonde floats down with a parachute. If someone finds the radiosonde, instructions tell him or her to mail it to the National Weather Service. But many are never returned.

Weather conditions miles above the Earth's surface are very important for forecasts. That information gives meteorologists clues about weather systems near the surface. For example, suppose forecasters locate a region of very low pressure several miles above the ground. This warns them a storm is likely to develop at the surface. Wind direction and air pressure high above the ground will guide the path of that storm. Knowing about upper-level weather is especially important for long-range forecasts. It helps meteorologists predict where storms will form, how strong they may become, and where they will travel.

Each weather station also scans for weather with Doppler radar. (This type of radar can measure the speed and direction of moving objects such as raindrops and snowflakes.)

COLORFUL AREAS ON THIS DOPPLER RADAR IMAGE SHOW A SEVERE THUNDERSTORM OVER KANSAS. THE RED AND ORANGE SPOTS SHOW THE MOST SEVERE WEATHER.

The radar scans the sky for several hundred miles. It shows where rain is falling and how heavy the rain is. It shows which way a storm is moving. Doppler radar also displays movement within a cloud. Spinning clouds may signal severe thunderstorms or tornadoes.

Sometimes scientists at a weather station see a severe storm forming on their radar screens. They check the direction it is moving. They trace the likely path of the storm using computers. Scientists then send alerts to local radio and TV stations. The alerts name towns in the storm's path. They warn people to take shelter.

ADVISORIES, WATCHES, AND WARNINGS

When severe weather may be on the way, the NWS alerts the public. It issues a watch, a warning, or an advisory.

A watch means dangerous storms are possible. For example, a thunderstorm watch tells people thunderstorms may develop.

A warning means a storm has been spotted. A severe thunderstorm warning means the weather station is tracking a dangerous storm that is expected to travel through the local area.

Advisories are used for less severe conditions. For example, wind advisories alert people if winds are blowing at 25 to 39 miles (40 to 63 km) per hour. A high wind warning is for winds of 40 miles (64 km) per hour or more.

The NWS also makes composite (combined) radar images. These images show data from many weather stations. A computer gathers the data and puts them together on a map of the United States. This map shows a radar image for the whole country.

Satellites track Earth's weather from space. Instruments and cameras aboard satellites record conditions on Earth and in the atmosphere. They send information and images back to Earth by radio.

Geostationary Operational Environmental Satellites (GOES) always remain above the same point on Earth's surface. These satellites travel in very high orbits (paths around Earth). They orbit about 22,000 miles (36,000 km) above the equator (an imaginary line around the middle of Earth). They monitor a large part of Earth's surface.

Geostationary satellites take digital photographs that show what Earth would look like to our own eyes from space.

SEE FOR YOURSELF:

You can see GOES images at the NWS website, http://www.weather.gov. The images show the day's weather. They are the same images forecasters use. You could use them to help make your own forecasts.

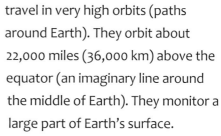

THIS IS PART OF THE SPACECRAFT THAT CARRIED A GEOSTATIONARY OPERATIONAL ENVIRONMENTAL SATELLITE INTO ORBIT IN 2006.

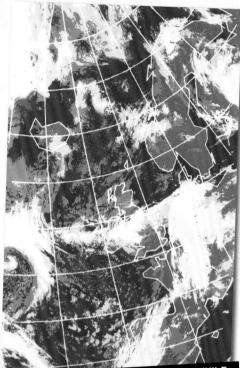

A GOES SATELLITE TOOK THIS IMAGE WHILE FLYING OVER WESTERN EUROPE. THE WHITE BANDS ARE CLOUDS. BLUE AND GREEN HAVE BEEN ADDED TO SHOW LAND AND SEA.

The photos show clouds and storms above Earth. In the photos, thin clouds look light gray. Thicker clouds—which bring rain and storms—look bright white from above. Forecasters can use the photos to watch storms as they move across Earth's surface.

The satellites also take images that show infrared radiation. Infrared radiation is heat. Infrared images show temperatures in the atmosphere. On these black-and-white pictures, black shows warm areas. White shows cold areas. Clouds—which are cooler than the ground below—appear gray or white. Computers add color to show the coldest cloud tops, where clouds are thickest and storms are usually strongest.

Geostationary satellites also take images that show water vapor (the gas form of water) in the air. In these pictures, areas of dry air appear black. The brightest white regions have the highest humidity. More water vapor means more clouds and storms.

Geostationary satellites always orbit above the equator. They can't see the polar regions well. So meteorologists need other satellites. These are Polar Orbiting Environmental Satellites (POES).

They circle Earth along north-south paths. Earth spins beneath them as they travel.

Polar orbiting satellites circle Earth about 530 miles (850 km) above the surface. They are much closer to the surface than geostationary satellites. They see the weather in more detail. On each orbit, POES satellites scan a different section of Earth. They survey most of Earth's surface twice each day.

ANALYZING WEATHER INFORMATION

Before making a forecast, meteorologists must analyze all the weather information collected at one time. At NWS headquarters near Washington, D.C., powerful supercomputers collect weather data from all NWS weather stations. They collect information on temperature, wind speed and direction, humidity, precipitation, and much more. They chart all this data on highly detailed, computerized weather maps. The computers draw new maps four times a day.

These meteorologists analyze a weather map at the NWS office in Washington, D.C., to track a storm.

Forecasters at local stations can look at the maps from NWS headquarters to see what's happening around the country. They also use their station's radar and get detailed information from other nearby weather stations and airports. Forecasters look at the latest satellite photos too.

Does this sound complicated? It is! Scientists at each station need plenty of information to make their forecasts. But NWS computers are powerful and fast. They help forecasters make sense of it all. The forecasters use their own judgment too. They have studied meteorology in school and have had years of practice making predictions. Over time, they learn from their successes and mistakes.

CAREERS IN METEOROLOGY

Would you like to be a meteorologist? Several thousand weather scientists work for the NWS. They work at weather stations and centers. They study the weather each day and make forecasts for their region.

Some meteorologists work for private companies. Airlines need weather information. So do big agriculture companies and other businesses. Many TV forecasters are trained meteorologists too.

Some meteorologists work at colleges. They teach students about the science of Earth's weather. And they do research. They study the world's weather and climates (regional weather patterns) to understand them better.

If you want to be a meteorologist, study hard. You'll need four years of college, including a lot of math and science classes. Then you'll need several more years to get a graduate degree in meteorology.

| CHAPTER TWO |

READING A WEATHER MAP

A weather map is a snapshot of the weather at a certain moment. Weather maps can show a whole continent or a small region. The maps show a lot of information.

Weather maps often show air pressure. A capital *L* on a map stands for a low pressure center (the point with the lowest air pressure in a region). The *L* is ordinarily printed in red. A high pressure center is shown by a capital *H*. It is usually blue.

Rain
Rain
Snow
Rain
Snow
Rain
Heavy Snow Possible
Rain/T'Storms
Rain/T'Storms
Severe T'Storms
NOAA
Flooding Possible

This map shows areas of high (H) and low (L) pressure. Low pressure conditions often bring storms.

FASCINATING FACT:

Weather maps are also called synoptic charts. A synopsis is a summary. Synoptic charts summarize the weather.

Air pressure affects winds and storms. Large, spinning storms called cyclones form around low pressure. North of the equator, cyclones spin counterclockwise around low pressure. Cyclones spin clockwise south of the equator. Winds also circle around high pressure centers, which have fair weather. These winds circle in the opposite direction from cyclone winds.

Scientists measure air pressure in millibars. Often, where air pressure is low, the weather is stormy. Where the pressure is high, the weather is usually fair. Average fair-weather pressure at sea level is about 1,013 millibars. (That is equal to about 30 inches [760 millimeters] of mercury—another unit sometimes used to measure air pressure.)

Some weather maps have thin, curved lines called isobars. Every point on an isobar has the same air pressure. Isobars are labeled in millibars. For example, every place along an isobar labeled 1020 has air pressure of 1,020 millibars.

Sometimes isobars are close together on a map. This means the air pressure in that region is changing quickly. Winds in that area will be strong. Where isobars are spread far apart, the wind will be gentle.

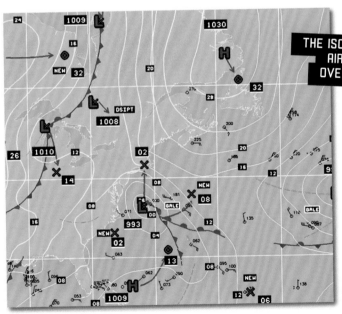

THE ISOBARS ON THIS MAP SHOW THE AIR PRESSURE, IN MILLIBARS, OVER NORTH AMERICA AND THE ATLANTIC OCEAN.

Weather maps may include isotherms too. An isotherm is also a curved line. Every point on it has the same temperature. An isotherm often shows where the temperature is 32°F (0°C). That's an important temperature to know—it's the freezing point of water. This isotherm is a dashed line. On the warmer side of it, precipitation (moisture that falls to the ground) is likely to fall as rain. Snow or sleet is more likely on the colder side.

The 0°F (about –18°C) isotherm appears on many winter weather maps. It alternates dashes and dots. This isotherm shows where weather is severely cold.

Fronts are another common part of weather maps. A front is a zone where different air masses—such as a warm air mass and a cold

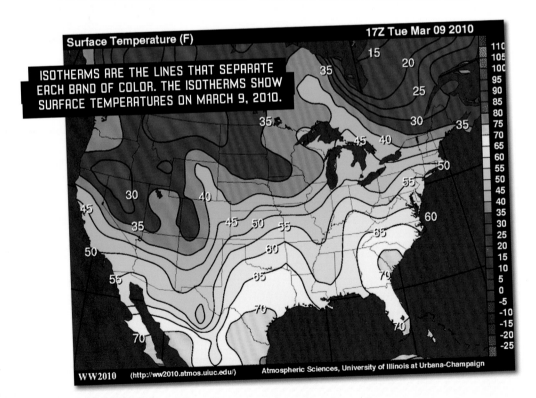

ISOTHERMS ARE THE LINES THAT SEPARATE EACH BAND OF COLOR. THE ISOTHERMS SHOW SURFACE TEMPERATURES ON MARCH 9, 2010.

THE HEAT INDEX AND WINDCHILL INDEX

We sweat to cool our bodies. But when the air is humid, sweat evaporates slowly. We don't cool off easily. Humidity makes us feel even hotter. Meteorologists use the heat index (or comfort index) to show this effect. Suppose the temperature is 90°F (32°C) and the humidity is 60 percent. The heat index says it feels like 100°F (38°C). In this way, the heat index warns people when it's dangerously hot and humid.

Wind can make the temperature feel cooler than it really is. The wind carries heat away from our skin. In winter that makes us feel colder. Forecasters use another scale to warn of dangerous cold. It's called the windchill index. Suppose the temperature is 32°F (0°C). If the wind is blowing at 25 miles (40 km) per hour, it would feel like 19°F (–8°C).

air mass—push against each other. When air masses meet, warmer air rises above colder air. The warm air cools. Water vapor in the air forms tiny liquid drops, which become clouds, rain, and snow. So weather along a front is often stormy.

On a map, a front is shown by a line. But the actual front covers a wide area. Cold fronts may be 50 miles (80 km) wide or more. Warm fronts can be hundreds of miles wide.

Cold Front

Warm Front

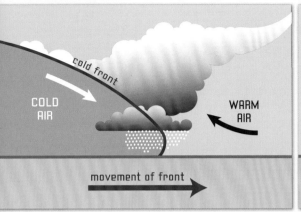

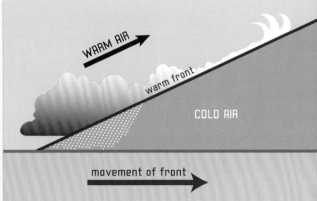

When cold air pushes under warmer air, a cold front forms. On the map, a cold front is a line of triangles. It is often printed in blue. The triangles point in the direction the front is moving.

A warm front forms when warm air moves over colder air. A warm front is shown on a map by a line of half circles. It is often printed in red. The half circles point in the direction the front is moving.

Sometimes two air masses sit side by side. Neither one can push the other out of the way. This is a stationary front. It appears on a map as a line of alternating triangles and half circles. The half circles point in one direction. The triangles point in the other. The line may be printed in alternating red and blue.

When a fast-moving cold front catches up to a slower-moving warm front, it is called an occluded front. In an occluded front, warm air is squeezed up above two colder air masses—the cold air that was ahead of the warm front and the cold air that caught up to the warm front. A map may show this front as a line of purple triangles and half circles. Or it may be a line of alternating blue triangles and red half circles. The shapes all point in the same direction. They show which way the front is moving.

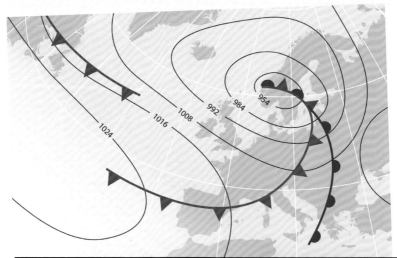

BLUE TRIANGLES AND RED SEMICIRCLES INDICATE COLD AND WARM FRONTS ON THIS WEATHER MAP. WHERE THE WARM FRONT AND COLD FRONT ARE JOINED, AN OCCLUDED FRONT HAS FORMED.

Weather maps show the locations of weather stations too. A small circle marks each station. If the circle is open, that means the sky there is clear. A filled circle means the sky is cloudy. A partly filled circle shows how much of the sky is covered with clouds.

Symbols and numbers around each circle make up a weather station plot. They describe the weather at the station. A wind flag, or wind barb, points into the circle.

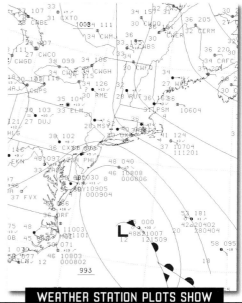

WEATHER STATION PLOTS SHOW TEMPERATURE, CLOUD COVER, WIND SPEED AND DIRECTION, AND MORE FOR THE NORTHEASTERN UNITED STATES.

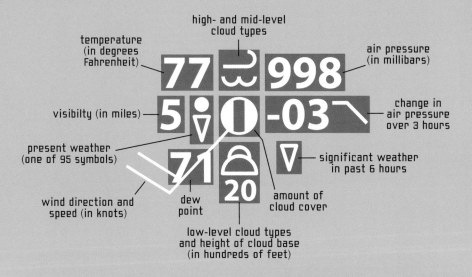

high- and mid-level cloud types

temperature (in degrees Fahrenheit)

air pressure (in millibars)

visibilty (in miles)

change in air pressure over 3 hours

present weather (one of 95 symbols)

significant weather in past 6 hours

wind direction and speed (in knots)

dew point

amount of cloud cover

low-level cloud types and height of cloud base (in hundreds of feet)

Many station plots on maps show less information, but a complete station plot like this tells a lot about the weather.

It points in the direction the wind is blowing. If the flag points into the circle from the west, the wind is blowing from the west. The lines at the end of the wind barb show the speed of the wind.

Other information may be printed around the circle too. Temperature is printed at the upper left. Precipitation symbols are just below the temperature. Symbols directly above and below the circle show the types of clouds over the station. Air pressure is usually shown on the right. The dew point—the temperature at which water vapor in the air will form dew or frost—may be at lower left. (This indicates how humid the air is.) Other data are also printed around the circle.

Forecasters need all those facts. But most people don't. So weather maps in the newspaper or on TV are much simpler. They leave out a lot of information.

CHAPTER THREE

MAKING A PREDICTION

Suppose you want to know what the weather will be in five minutes. That should be easy. Just look outside. Is it sunny? It will probably be sunny in five minutes. Is it cold? It will probably still be cold.

How about an hour from now? That's a little harder. Weather can change more in an hour. You would need more information to make this forecast. Let's say the wind is blowing from the south. You'll need to know about the weather south of you. It's probably headed your way.

You'll need to know if the temperature and air pressure are rising or falling. Is the humidity changing? Each change is another clue about the weather to come.

Predicting tomorrow's weather is even tougher. In twenty-four hours, the weather could change a lot. You'll need much more information to make a forecast. How about next week's weather? That prediction is very hard. Even meteorologists aren't certain about weather that far in the future.

To make a forecast, meteorologists look at current conditions. They also study the NWS computers. The computer programs they use are called atmospheric models, or weather models. The models use weather data from around the world. They predict how the weather will change. The computer draws its forecasts as weather maps showing future conditions.

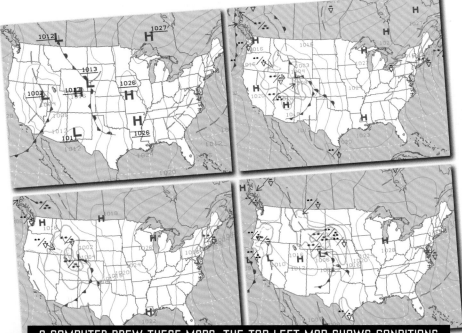

A COMPUTER DREW THESE MAPS. THE TOP LEFT MAP SHOWS CONDITIONS AT THE TIME THE MAPS WERE DRAWN. THE OTHER MAPS SHOW FORECASTS FOR TWELVE HOURS LATER (*top right*), TWENTY-FOUR HOURS LATER (*bottom left*), AND FORTY-EIGHT HOURS LATER (*bottom right*).

WEATHER INDICATORS

A few signs can help you make your own forecast.

Air pressure:
- Steady or rising air pressure above 1,016 millibars (30 inches of mercury): fair weather
- Falling pressure, or pressure below 1,008 millibars (29.8 inches): increasing clouds and rain

Clouds:
- Thickening altostratus and stratus clouds (flat, gray clouds that cover the sky): a coming warm front; possible rain or snow
- Large, rapidly building white cumulus clouds: thunderstorms possible
- Clear night sky: temperatures will drop overnight; heavy dew or frost
- Cloud-covered night sky: temperatures won't fall much overnight; little dew or frost

Winds:
- Brisk wind from the west or northwest: high pressure moving in. Expect fair skies and low humidity.
- Winds from the south or southeast: rising temperatures and humidity. A warm front may bring clouds and rain.

The computer draws a map for twelve to seventy-two hours into the future. Each map is called a prog, short for prognostic chart. The further into the future a map shows, the less certain it is to be right. Progs become much less reliable when they predict weather three days or more in advance.

Forecasters at each local weather station look at the progs on their computers, along with their own station's weather data and radar and satellite images. Forecasters use two or more different computer screens. This system lets them compare progs from different models. Sometimes the models agree. When that happens, it's fairly easy to make a forecast.

But sometimes the models don't agree. One model might predict a storm moving up the east coast of the United States. Another could show that same storm drifting over the Atlantic Ocean.

When models disagree, forecasters rely on their experience. They compare the current conditions with familiar weather patterns. Then they make the best forecast they can. The forecast may even mention that the models disagree.

A HURRICANE SPECIALIST AT THE NATIONAL HURRICANE CENTER IN MIAMI, FLORIDA, STUDIES MODELS AND RADAR IMAGES TO CHART THE COURSE OF TROPICAL STORM ALBERTO IN 2006.

7 DAY PLANNER

THU	FRI	SAT	SUN	MON	TUE	WED
☀	⛅	⛅	☁	☁	☀	☀
PERFECT!	WINDY	CHANGING	50%	80%	MILD	MILD
76	74	66	62	62	73	75
55	53	48	43	43	52	54

COMPUTER MODELS HELP METEOROLOGISTS MAKE EXTENDED FORECASTS. THIS SEVEN-DAY FORECAST SHOWS THE PREDICTED DAILY HIGH AND LOW TEMPERATURES, CLOUD COVER, AND CHANCE OF RAIN (AS A PERCENTAGE). BUT THE FURTHER OUT THE PREDICTION, THE LESS CERTAIN IT IS TO BE ACCURATE.

SHORT- AND LONG-RANGE FORECASTS

A forecast may be one of four types: very short range, short range, medium range, or long range. Very short-range forecasts cover the next six hours. Meteorologists use radar and information from local weather stations to make these forecasts. Satellite images also help. These forecasts are very reliable.

Short-range forecasts cover six to sixty hours. That's up to two and a half days. To make these predictions, forecasters use current conditions and computer progs. They also look at satellite images. Short-range forecasts are usually quite accurate too.

Medium-range forecasts cover three days to about a week. They are also called extended forecasts. These forecasts are made mostly with computer models. They are less accurate than short-range predictions. Forecasters often change them as days go by.

Long-range forecasts are called outlooks. They give a broad picture of weather for one to three months. An outlook is based on conditions around the world at the time it's made. Scientists look at weather patterns from past years. Ocean temperatures, which affect the air above the water, are important too. Outlooks don't try to predict weather for any one day. They just compare the expected conditions in the coming months to thirty-year averages for the same months. For example, a summer outlook might call for average rainfall and above average temperatures.

The National Hurricane Center also issues outlooks each year. They tell whether the coming storm season is expected to involve storms of normal, above-normal, or below-normal strength.

ACCURACY AND SKILL

Modern weather forecasts are usually quite accurate. Short-range forecasts are almost always on target. But forecasters sometimes make mistakes.

How accurate should a forecast be? Suppose it's mid-July. The forecast calls for a high of 90°F (32°C). What if it hits 92°F (33°C)? That's pretty close. Was the forecast right? What if the temperature is a degree warmer than that? Or two? How far off must a forecast be before we say it was wrong?

Unfortunately, there isn't one right answer to that question. Meteorologists don't have a method to decide if a forecast was right or wrong. But they can judge forecasting *skill*. A skilled forecast is more accurate and precise than what you could predict just by knowing the typical weather.

Here's an example. Suppose you were in Phoenix, Arizona. Phoenix is in the desert. You could predict "sunny and dry" each day. You'd be right almost every time. But you wouldn't be using skill. A skilled forecaster can predict those few days when Phoenix gets clouds or rain.

The area around Phoenix, Arizona, gets only about 8 inches (20 centimeters) of rain each year. So most days there are sunny and dry.

These beachgoers were probably expecting a hot, sunny day. But dark clouds are moving in.

WHY DO FORECASTS GO WRONG?

Sometimes forecasters call for a sunny day, and we get thundershowers instead. Or they predict rain, and we have only clouds.

Errors occur for many reasons. Computer models are very complex. After putting in the current weather conditions, meteorologists might run a program ten times. Each time, the results might be different. Forecasters then use the average results. But the average isn't guaranteed to be right either.

The computer models might miss something important. Models don't use every possible bit of information. For example, they don't include local details. So they wouldn't take a small lake into account. But lakes stay cool in summer. They hold heat in winter. They put water vapor into the air. All those things affect local weather.

MAKE YOUR OWN FORECASTS

Why not make your own weather predictions? You can collect some weather measurements at home.

Use an outdoor thermometer to check air temperature. You'll need to record air pressure and humidity too. If you have a barometer *(right)* and a hygrometer at home to measure those, check them each day. If not, use data from the nearest airport or weather station. You can find data on the NWS website or the website of a TV station or newspaper. Your weather station might also include a wind vane and an anemometer to measure wind speed and direction. You could also get those measurements from a weather station. Or find instructions in a book or online to make your own instruments!

Set your instruments in a shady, open spot outdoors. Record your daily readings in a journal. Then write down your forecast. Later, you can compare your prediction with the next day's weather. See how skillful a forecaster you become!

Models don't cover the whole planet either. Computers are just not powerful enough. So each model covers a region. Conditions outside the region affect the weather. But the model can't predict that.

Finally, weather is never perfectly predictable. It's just too complicated. A small event in one place can have a big effect somewhere else. For example, consider a thermal. A thermal is a rising bubble of warm air. It can rise 3,300 feet (1,000 m) and become a puffy cumulus cloud. The cloud might keep growing and become a thunderstorm. It could affect weather hundreds of miles away. Or the cloud could just evaporate (turn from liquid droplets into water vapor) and disappear. There's no way to be sure in advance.

CHAPTER FOUR

PREDICTING CLIMATE CHANGE

Climate describes a region's typical weather. Scientists measure climate over many years. Climate includes average and record temperatures, rainfall, typical storms, and seasonal changes. For instance, a desert climate is hot and dry, while a tropical climate is hot and wet.

Some weather scientists focus on studying the climate instead of daily forecasts. They study long-term changes in Earth's atmosphere and weather patterns.

You probably have heard about climate change in the news. But climate change is nothing new. Earth's climate is always changing.

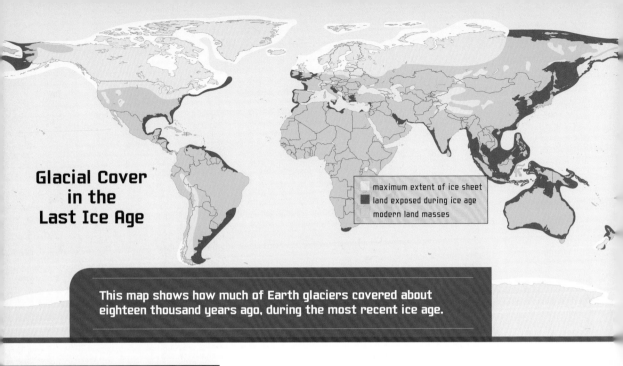

Glacial Cover in the Last Ice Age

maximum extent of ice sheet

land exposed during ice age

modern land masses

This map shows how much of Earth glaciers covered about eighteen thousand years ago, during the most recent ice age.

FASCINATING FACT:

A forecast usually shows the chance of rain as a percentage. Suppose there's a 50 percent chance of rain. Does that mean it will rain half the time? No.

It means that any spot covered by the forecast has a 50 percent chance of getting some rainfall—and an equal chance of getting none at all.

At times in the past, the world's climate was much colder. During several ice ages, glaciers (thick sheets of ice) covered much of Earth's land. At other times, Earth's climate was warmer. A thousand years ago, Greenland had trees growing on it. In modern times, it is covered in glaciers.

Rainfall patterns change too. Deserts can shrink or expand. So can rain forests.

Many things can cause climate change. Earth's orbit is not perfectly regular. Earth's angle and distance from the sun vary. Over thousands of years, this variation can change climates. Such changes may have caused past ice ages.

The sun's output isn't perfectly steady either. Sometimes the sun produces a bit more energy than other times. Sunspots are huge magnetic storms on the sun's surface. The number of sunspots goes up and down every eleven years. Earth's temperature seems to increase with the number of sunspots. Rising temperatures can lead to drought (rain shortage).

Volcanoes can affect climate too. When they erupt, they put dust and gas into the air. The dust blocks sunlight from reaching Earth. A large eruption may cool Earth by a degree or more for several years.

FASCINATING FACT:

Mount Tambora, a volcano in Indonesia, erupted in 1815. The dust it threw into the atmosphere probably caused the "Year without a Summer" in 1816. That year, New England had snowstorms in June. The cold killed crops, causing food shortages.

Volcanic explosions send particles into the air that can affect Earth's climate.

Climate change usually happens slowly. As the climate changes, some animals and plants may move to other areas to find the climate they need. Other plant and animals species adapt to live in the new climate by changing their diets or breeding patterns.

But recently, Earth's climate seems to be changing quickly. This change is known as global warming. Average temperatures have risen about 1°F (0.6°C) since 1900. That may not seem like a lot. But it is much faster than temperatures had been changing for the thousands of years before then. If Earth keeps warming, it will be hard for some plants and animals to adapt quickly enough to survive.

THE EXHAUST FROM CARS AND TRUCKS INCLUDES CARBON DIOXIDE, A GREENHOUSE GAS. SCIENTISTS THINK THE EXTRA CARBON DIOXIDE IN THE AIR IS INCREASING THE GREENHOUSE EFFECT.

Most scientists think human activity is part of the cause of climate change. People are burning more fuel than ever to drive cars, run factories, and heat and cool their homes. Burning fuels such as oil, coal, and natural gas puts greenhouse gases such as carbon dioxide into the air. These gases hold heat in Earth's atmosphere. They act like glass in a greenhouse, letting light in and trapping the energy as heat. Adding carbon dioxide to the air adds to the greenhouse effect.

Most scientists think Earth's climate will keep getting warmer throughout the twenty-first century. By the year 2100, average temperatures could be 2 to 8°F (about 1 to 4.5°C) higher than they were in 2000. That's a very wide range of predictions. That tells us how uncertain climate forecasts are. Different parts of Earth will warm at different rates. The greatest warming will probably be near the North Pole and the South Pole.

As the climate gets warmer, polar ice and glaciers are likely to melt. Sea levels will rise as the melting ice floods into oceans. Some people predict a rise of more than 20 inches (0.5 meters) by the end of the twenty-first century. Some predict more. The rising seas would flood coastal lands. High waves from storms would damage coastlines.

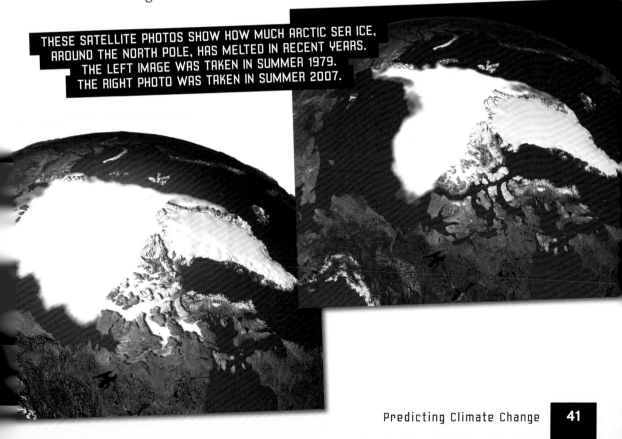

THESE SATELLITE PHOTOS SHOW HOW MUCH ARCTIC SEA ICE, AROUND THE NORTH POLE, HAS MELTED IN RECENT YEARS. THE LEFT IMAGE WAS TAKEN IN SUMMER 1979. THE RIGHT PHOTO WAS TAKEN IN SUMMER 2007.

Climate change could create new weather patterns. Some regions would get more rain. Others would get less. This change would affect crops. Storms might be more severe. Insects that thrive in warm weather could move to new places. They might bring insectborne diseases, such as malaria, with them and spread such diseases more widely.

However, no one knows exactly how much the climate will change. Climate is very complicated. For example, more water evaporates into the air during warm weather than during cold weather. Water vapor is a greenhouse gas. It holds heat in the atmosphere. But water vapor also forms clouds. And clouds reflect sunlight back into space. That makes Earth cooler. So as the air gets warmer, more clouds might help make it cool again. Facts like this make climate change very hard to predict.

Human behavior can also change. We could use energy more wisely. We could conserve energy in our homes. We may find ways to reduce greenhouse gases from car and factory exhaust. And using more water and wind power would put fewer greenhouse gases into the air.

Plants also absorb carbon dioxide. If people cut down fewer trees—and planted more—carbon dioxide levels could fall or at least rise more slowly. All these actions could reduce global warming.

How will Earth's climate change in the next one hundred years? In part, the answer depends on how we live our lives. In the meantime, studying the weather has become more important for us all.

FORECASTING FOLKLORE

Hundreds of folk sayings predict the weather. Some are based on scientific fact. Others are not helpful at all. Here are a few useful sayings based on science.

Red sky at night, sailors' delight: If it's dry to the west, with no more than a few fair-weather clouds, we see a reddish sunset. (Otherwise, western clouds might block the sunset.) Most weather in North America comes from the west. So if the sky to the west is clear—with a red sunset—the next day's weather is likely to be fair. That's good for sailing or anything else.

Look for rain when birds fly low: High air pressure helps birds fly more easily. Air under high pressure is more dense. So birds get more lift when they flap their wings. Low pressure brings rain and storms. So birds may fly lower when rain is coming.

Sticky door, rain will pour: Wood absorbs moisture from humid air. Moist wooden doors swell and stick. And when the air is humid, rain is more likely.

A halo around the sun *(right)* **or moon means rain or snow is coming soon:** Sometimes we see a ring of icy cirrostratus clouds around the sun or moon. These clouds come ahead of warm fronts. And warm fronts often bring rain or snow.

Clear moon, frost soon: Clouds act like a blanket above Earth. They hold in heat. On cloudy nights, Earth's surface stays warm. When the night sky is clear, heat releases into space. Earth's surface cools more quickly. Dew or frost might form on cold nights.

GLOSSARY

air pressure: the force of air pushing evenly in all directions against any object

anemometer: a device that measures wind speed

atmosphere: the blanket of gases that surrounds Earth's surface

barometer: an instrument that measures air pressure

buoy: a device that floats in the water, usually anchored in place. Weather buoys carry instruments to measure weather conditions.

climate: the average weather or typical weather patterns of a region

climate change: long-term changes in Earth's weather patterns and averages

cyclone: a region of low pressure with winds that circle counterclockwise in the Northern Hemisphere. Cyclones usually produce storms.

dew point: the temperature at which water vapor in the air condenses into liquid. The dew point is a measure of humidity.

forecast: a prediction of future weather

front: the zone where two different air masses meet

global warming: the recent rise in the average temperature of Earth's lower atmosphere. Most scientists think this is due to more heat-trapping gases in the atmosphere.

greenhouse effect: the natural process by which the atmosphere traps heat near Earth's surface, keeping the heat from escaping into space

greenhouse gases: gases, including water vapor and carbon dioxide, that hold heat in the atmosphere

humidity: the amount of water vapor in the air

hygrometer: a device that measures relative humidity

isobar: a line on a weather map that shows locations with the same air pressure

isotherm: a dashed line on a weather map that shows locations with the same temperature

meteorologist: a scientist who studies weather and climate

outlook: a long-range weather prediction that covers one to three months

prog: a computer-drawn weather map that predicts future weather conditions. Prog is short for "prognostic chart."

radar: a device that locates distant objects, such as moisture droplets, using radio waves. Doppler radar can also measure speed and direction.

radiosonde: a package of weather instruments carried beneath a weather balloon

rain gauge: a device that measures the amount of rain that has fallen

satellite: a machine in orbit around Earth

supercomputer: a very fast computer with huge amounts of memory and computing power

thermometer: a device that measures temperature

weather: the current condition of the atmosphere

weather model: also called atmospheric model; a computer program that collects weather data and uses it to predict future changes in the weather

weather station: a center with a set of instruments for measuring and recording weather conditions, including temperature, air pressure, wind speed and direction, and rainfall

wind barb: a symbol on a weather map that shows wind direction and speed

wind vane: a device that indicates wind direction

SELECTED BIBLIOGRAPHY

Aguardo, Edward, and James E. Burt. *Understanding Weather & Climate.* 3rd ed. Upper Saddle River, NJ: Prentice Hall, 2004.

Ahrens, C. Donald. *Meteorology Today.* 8th ed. Belmont, CA: Thompson Higher Education, 2007.

Allaby, Michael. *The Facts on File Weather and Climate Handbook.* New York: Facts on File, 2002.

Dunlop, Storm. *Weather.* New York: HarperCollins, 2006.

Lutgens, Frederick and Edward J. Tarbuck. *The Atmosphere: An Introduction to Meteorology.* 10th ed. Upper Saddle River, NJ: Prentice Hall, 2006.

Mayes, Julian. *Understanding Weather: A Visual Approach.* New York: Oxford University Press, 2004.

FURTHER READING

Allaby, Michael. *DK Guide to Weather.* New York: DK Pub., 2006. Lots of vivid photos and information are packed into this book to help readers explore the various aspects of weather.

Carson, Mary Kay. *Weather Projects for Young Scientists: Experiments and Science Fair Ideas.* Chicago: Chicago Review Press, 2007. This book offers comprehensive weather-related activities, putting a fun spin on learning about the weather.

Johnson, Rebecca L. *Satellites.* Minneapolis: Lerner Publications Company, 2006. Get an in-depth look at satellites through the many facts and real-life photos this book has to offer.

Mattern, Joanne. *Can Lightning Strike the Same Place Twice?* Minneapolis: Lerner Publications Company, 2010. Check out this book to find out the facts: are all of those myths you've been told about Earth, the weather, and the environment true? Mattern exposes the truth about seventeen of these commonly heard statements.

Rodgers, Alan, and Angella Streluk. *Forecasting the Weather*. Chicago: Heinemann Library, 2007. This book gives a detailed introduction to the technology, the terms, and the processes behind weather forecasting.

WEBSITES

NOAA's National Weather Service
http://www.nws.noaa.gov/
Visit this site for information on U.S. weather conditions, weather maps and models, and forecasts from very short term to outlooks.

The Weather Channel
http://www.weather.com/
Visit this site to find out the day's weather predictions for any city in the country!

Weather Forecasting: Online Meteorology Guide
http://ww2010.atmos.uiuc.edu/(Gh)/guides/mtr/fcst/home.rxml
Check out this site to learn exactly how weather forecasters predict the weather and all of the factors involved in meteorology.

Web Weather for Kids
http://eo.ucar.edu/webweather/
Click on "Predict the Weather!" for forecasting tips.

INDEX

ABOUT THE AUTHOR

Paul Fleisher is a veteran educator and the author of dozens of science titles for children, including the Secrets of the Universe series, the Early Bird Food Web series, and *The Big Bang* and *Evolution* for the Great Ideas of Science series. He is also the author of *Parasites: Latching On to a Free Lunch.* He lives with his wife in Richmond, Virginia.

PHOTO ACKNOWLEDGMENTS

The images in this book are used with the permission of: © Dennis MacDonald/Alamy, pp. 1, 19; Eric Kurth, NOAA/NWS/ER/WFO/Sacramento, p. 3; © Stephen Morton/Stringer/ Getty Images, p. 4; AP Photo/Richard Drew, p. 5; © Scientifica/Visuals Unlimited, Inc., p. 6; © Steve Allen/The Image Bank/Getty Images, p. 8; © Digital Zoo/Photodisc/Getty Images, p. 9; Courtesy of the National Oceanic and Atmospheric Administration, pp. 10, 20, 21, 25 (bottom), 28 (all); © Jim Edds/Photo Researchers, Inc., p. 11; © David R. Frazier/Photolibrary, Inc./Photo Researchers, Inc., p. 12; © Jim Reed/Photo Researchers, Inc., p. 13; © Ilene MacDonald/Alamy, p. 14; NASA Kennedy Space Center, p. 15; © University of Dundee/ Photo Researchers, Inc., p. 16; Christopher Strong/NOAA, p. 17; © WW2010, Department of Atmospheric Sciences, University of Illinois at Urbana-Champaign, p. 22; © Laura Westlund/ Independent Picture Service, pp. 24, 26; © Dorling Kindersley/Getty Images, p. 25 (top); © David De Lossy/Digital Vision/Getty Images, p. 27; © Philippe Colombi/Photodisc/Getty Images, p. 29; © Joe Raedle/Stringer/Getty Images, p. 30; Courtesy: KSTP-TV, LLC, p. 31; © Anna Cavallo, p. 33; © Barry Lewis/Alamy, p. 34; © Steve Cole/Photolibrary, p. 35; © Daisy Gilardini/Taxi/Getty Images, p. 37; © Bill Hauser/Independent Picture Service, p. 38; © Dr. Richard Roscoe/Visuals Unlimited, Inc., p. 39; © Gemphotography/Dreamstime.com, p. 40; NASA/GSFC, p. 41 (both); © Stocktrek Images/Getty Images, p. 43.

Front cover: © Getty Images.